Know Your Bird Sounds
COMMON WESTERN SPECIES

Know Your Bird Sounds
COMMON WESTERN SPECIES

Kevin Colver
and Lang Elliott

photos by Brian E. Small

STACKPOLE BOOKS

Published by
STACKPOLE BOOKS
5067 Ritter Road
Mechanicsburg, PA 17055
www.stackpolebooks.com

Printed in China

10 9 8 7 6 5 4 3 2 1

First edition

Library of Congress Cataloging-in-Publication Data

Colver, Kevin J.
  Know your bird sounds : common western species / Kevin Colver and Lang Elliott. — 1st ed.
      p. cm.
    ISBN 0-8117-3446-3
  1. Birdsongs—West (U.S.) 2. Birds—Vocalization—West (U.S.) 3. Songbirds—West (U.S.) I. Elliott, Lang. II. Title.

QL698.5.C65 2008
598.159'40978—dc22

                                                    2007032244

    ISBN 978-0-8117-3446-2

Contents

Preface

I t's five-thirty in the morning, aspen leaves shimmer with the slightest breeze, and the sun is about to erupt from behind a distant ridge to the east. I'm in full camo, sitting motionless among the purple lupine, a bit back from my stereo microphone. An American Robin has already been at it for forty-five minutes, joined early on by a Western Wood-pewee. And now a Dusky Flycatcher, Warbling Vireos, Audubon's Warbler, and the resident White-crowned Sparrow are filling my earphones with song. Another June dawn chorus is in full swing.

Why do I record birds? I don't know that I'll ever be able to really say for sure, but the experience fills me—I am immersed; I am home. There is a power swaying and pulsing like the rhythm of deep waves rocking a kelp forest. I float with the power like a drifting fish, unconsciously allowing the back and forth rhythms to carry me. Trees, grass, ants crawling across my boot—I am in resonance with them this morning.

All around me, nature's natural rhythms are in force. A pair of woodpeckers are preparing a nest cavity in the old aspen in front of me. A weasel explores the fallen log a few feet away from me before moving on, never aware of my presence. A few years ago, just over this ridge and at this same hour, I watched a cougar kill a mule deer doe about fifty yards from me. The doe agonized before she succumbed; her fearful fawn ran right up to me, then ran off. I backed away, and the big cat never detected me.

Listening to each recording I made brings back fragments of the feelings I had when I made it. Sound conjures up memories in ways that photos can't. The whine of cicada in Big Bend National Park, wetlands alive with the tremendous din of Marsh Wrens and Yellow-headed Blackbirds, the delicate song of a Horned Lark in a flat wasteland I had nearly passed over—the sounds allow me to relive the experiences.

With this book and CD, I want to share with you a taste of that which I love. This is a sampler, an introduction to the bird sounds of western North America. My quest for new sounds will last a lifetime. I'm happy to share these memories with you.

K. C.

Introduction

This book and CD begin with a climb into the Rocky Mountains, after which we descend into the western foothills and move through the Great Basin sagebrush and juniper desert. We'll then travel south into western Texas, then east into Arizona, exploring the Chihuahuan and Sonoran Deserts. From there, we'll go to California's beaches, mountains, and redwood forests, then move up into the Pacific temperate rain forests. Wetland areas scattered throughout the West will round out our tour.

Each recording included here was made with state-of-the-art digital recording equipment. The recordings of particular species include the sounds of other species in the background, presenting a more realistic picture and offering additional identification challenges. This package makes no attempt to present a complete picture of all the birds of western North America—to do so would necessarily include some six hundred speices. We tried to include the most common and some of the most interesting sounds here.

1. Mountain Chickadee

Poecile gambeli

Winter or summer, the Mountain Chickadee always seems cheerful and busy. Watch for these tiny birds in conifers, aspen, Great Basin cedar, and pinon pine. Chickadees are constantly investigating twigs and bark for bits of insect prey. A white eyebrow stripe helps you quickly distinguish this species from others in the chickadee family.

The Mountain Chickadee's dry and raspy call is another distinguishing feature that takes some practice to differentiate from other chickadees'. It is often written as *chick-a-dee-dee* and serves as an alarm or scold call. The male Mountain Chickadee sings a lilting song, which can be thought of as a descending *fee-bee-bay*.

ine Siskins seem hyperactive as they chase each other through the pines. If you can get one to hold still long enough for observation you'll note the bird's brown and pale streaks, delicate bill, and a flash of yellow in its wings. Pinecone seeds are a favorite food, but the bird also eats seeds from other plants, insects, and food from feeders.

Spring is an especially active time for these tiny birds. Male Pine Siskins make varied warbled songs beginning in January and February, as winter flocks break up into smaller groups until pair bonds form. The group's courtship calls and songs often blend in rapid succession.

3. Red-breasted Nuthatch   *Sitta canadensis*

Any bird climbing headfirst down a tree trunk in the western mountains is likely to be a nuthatch, and the Red-breasted Nuthatch is the common nuthatch here. The bird's movements are distinctive: it usually starts at the top of a tree and works its way down, searching for insect prey in the bark, until it reaches the lower trunk. Then it flies to the top of the next tree and starts foraging again.

The Red-breasted Nuthatch's flat, monotone, beeping call is heard year-round but becomes incessant during early summer courtship. A male may call for several minutes nonstop as it shows off a potential nest cavity to its mate.

Nature's percussion section includes the Downy Woodpecker. This black-and-white bird, our smallest woodpecker, performs its snare drum roll on a resonant dead tree limb, its message reverberating through the forest. This display method allows a tiny performer to broadcast information over a large territory in a manner much more efficient than any vocal performance could achieve. The downy's drum sequence is steady and unbroken and is used to advertise its territory and attract a mate.

To show alarm or keep in contact with its mate, the Downy Woodpecker also makes a sharp *peek* call, heard often during its frequent visits to back-yard feeders.

*I*n the intermountain west, our common sapsucker is the Red-naped Sapsucker, a species closely related to the Yellow-bellied Sapsucker, of which it was once considered a subspecies. The Red-naped Sapsucker is distinguishable by its unbroken red throat patch that touches its white mustache stripe.

In any particular habitat, each woodpecker species will drum at its own rate per second. Thus woodpeckers can recognize others of their own species. Sapsuckers, however, overlap drum speed with neighboring woodpecker species. How do they recognize their own? By drumming out an irregular and syncopated beat instead of the standard regular drum roll used by most other species. Male sapsuckers also make a nasal screech.

A plain olive plumage belies the joyful, rolling, rhythmic song we hear from the Warbling Vireo. This bird will sing all day long and even into late summer when other bird species are falling silent. With such a busy singing schedule the male cannot afford to perch and sing all day. Instead, it will continue foraging for caterpillars through the aspen or cottonwood leaves, singing all the way. Males have been known to sing even as they brood their young.

The Warbling Vireo is paler and less yellow than other vireo species. It sports a faint white stripe above each eye.

7. Yellow-rumped Warbler   *Dendroica coronata*

A flash of yellow, bordered by elegant gray and black, alerts us to the Yellow-rumped Warbler. In most of the West, the Audubon's subspecies will predominate; it's easily distinguished by its yellow throat from the myrtle subspecies found in Alaska and the East, which has a white throat. The daily habits of this warbler include near-constant searching of twigs and branches for tiny insect and spider prey. It's an active bird found in a variety of habitats from pine forests to Pacific beaches.

The Yellow-rumped Warbler's song is a lively trill that seems to change pitch for the last few notes.

A first view of the Western Tanager is always a memorable event. The bird's flaming red and yellow plumage seems out of place in dark mountain forests. It has an almost tropical flair. And well it might—like all tanagers, Western Tanagers pass most of their lives in the tropics of Central and South America. No other tanager ventures as far north or into such cool mountain haunts as does the Western Tanager, however. Lucky bird-watchers occasionally see the bird visiting backyard feeders for fruit.

The tanager's *cheer-up, cheer-up, cheer-up* song sounds something like the American Robin's, although it is drier and less piercing.

S cientists have discovered that, early in its youth, a male White-crowned Sparrow learns its particular song by mimicking older males singing nearby. It will then sing the song it learns for the rest of his life. It's a fine example of avian musical "culture" being passed down from one generation to the next. And because the sparrow doesn't range very far, groups of white-crowns sometimes develop a local dialect; their songs are all sung in a specific way. The song is usually a mix of long and sliding notes and short notes.

The Lazuli Bunting is the predominant bunting of western mountain meadows and foothill brushland. The male sports a bright blue head and back, reddish chest, and whitish underbelly. White wing bars distinguish it from the similar Indigo Bunting. (The bird's name is associated with the rock known as lapis lazuli, which includes the blue mineral lazurite.) Scientists have learned that Lazuli Buntings stop in the middle of their migration to complete their autumn molt before moving on to their winter range in Mexico.

The bunting's striking plumage is matched by its rapid, enthusiastic song, which the male often sings while holding its wings open to attract a mate.

11. Dusky Flycatcher — *Empidonax oberholseri*

The Empidonax family of flycatchers have a justified reputation of being difficult to identify by sight in the field. But identifying the common Dusky Flycatcher—with its typical greenish gray and brownish gray plumage, faint wing bars, and white eye rings—becomes a tiny bit easier once we hear its squeaky, three-part song. Even then, though, it takes some practice to tell it apart from other local flycatchers.

Breeding habitat also gives us a useful identification clue. The Dusky Flycatcher prefers to nest in open foothill brush and mountain meadow edges. Many other flycatchers seem to like more forested nesting grounds.

12. Hermit Thrush
Catharus guttatus

At sunset, pure, ascending, and haunting notes drift through the woodlands. It's a Hermit Thrush, whose flutelike song—once famously written as *oh, holy, holy*—is often regarded as one of the most beautiful in the animal kingdom. A common resident of mountain forests, the Hermit Thrush is the only spotted thrush that spends the winter in North America.

The bird is somewhat secretive, but it can be seen foraging on the forest floor or low in the underbrush. When it's in view, it's best identified by its spotted breast and its habit of pumping its tail (which is distinctly reddish) up and down.

13. Yellow Warbler *Dendroica petechia*

The common and brightly colored Yellow Warbler is associated with water in much of the arid west. The bird spends much of its time foraging in the patches of trees and shrubs that grow next to streams and ponds on its summer breeding grounds. Shady cottonwoods, a trickling waterway, and singing Yellow Warblers are a refreshing combination on a sunny afternoon. It's no wonder the bird is sometimes nicknamed the "summer warbler."

The Yellow Warbler's song can be thought of as a prettily whistled *sweet, sweet, sweet, I'm so sweet.* Male warblers begin singing soon after arriving in the spring.

T he Western Meadowlark is a common resident of arid grasslands, farm country, and expanses of Great Basin desert. Perched on a fence post, the bird captures a splash of sunshine on its breast and salutes the rising sun with a series of expressive melodies. It can be distinguished from its eastern counterpart by its slightly paler coloration and rich, melodious song, which the male uses to loudly advertise its territory.

Meadowlarks are members of the Troupial family of birds and are related to blackbirds, orioles, grackles, and cowbirds. A ground nester, the bird loses important nesting sites when grasslands disappear.

Many visitors to the vast expanses of Great Basin sagebrush pass through quickly, stopping only long enough to get gas and drive on. It takes some time to get to know this country, but it is time well spent. There is a special feeling you get walking alone during sunrise, the sweet smell of sage in the air, surrounded on all sides by the song of the Brewer's Sparrow.

This bird sports unremarkable, drab plumage, but it can quickly be distinguished by its long and variable buzzy song. Unfortunately, Brewer's Sparrow populations appear to be in decline as more and more of their favorite habitat is developed.

16. Sage Sparrow
Amphispiza belli

The Sage Sparrow claims a large territory in western sagebrush country. Somewhat shy and difficult to see, the bird perches in the upper branches of the bush so it remains semihidden when it sings its subtle back-and-forth song. During a bout of singing, the sparrow roves amid the sagebrush, singing from one bush, then moving to another. It also spends much time on the ground.

Broken white eye rings, a distinct white spot in front of each eye, and a central breast spot are good field marks for the Sage Sparrow—if you can get a good look at one.

A bird of western dry brush, the lively Bewick's Wren is common throughout the Southwest and into California. In some cases, however, its population is declining because of competition over nest sites with the pugnacious House Wren. The Bewick's Wren is readily identifiable by its bold white eyebrow stripe and long tail, which it often holds high above its back.

The wren family is noted for being vocal, and the Bewick's Wren is no exception. It sings its loud and variable song from the tops of bushes and shrubs throughout its territory and has been known to sing in every season.

In general, birdsong has evolved so it is most effective in the bird's preferred habitat. Pure, flutelike notes transmit well through woodlands, but the open countryside requires coarse, buzzy, broadband notes that can be heard in the wind. The Lark Sparrow, a resident of grasslands that contain at least some trees and shrubs, uses both types of notes. Its complex song mixes distinct buzzes with melodic trills.

Extremely social, the Lark Sparrow moves in flocks even during nesting season. Its distinctive head markings and song distinguish it from other sparrows. Unlike most songbirds, it walks on the ground instead of hopping.

Vast expanses of open wasteland in the western desert are so dry that only scattered weeds and grasses a few inches tall can survive. Yet this barren land is home to the western race of the Horned Lark, a common bird that is often thought of as rare by those who avoid its desolate habitat.

During cool spring mornings and evenings, the Horned Lark sings a tinkly song from any slight rise in the flat landscape. Its fluttering display flight—in which the bird circles high in the air before plummeting rapidly, pulling up just before it reaches the ground—is spectacular.

T he Cactus Wren is the poster bird for southwestern deserts; it's also the state bird of Arizona. The largest of the wrens, it has speckled plumage, bold white eyebrow stripes, and a long curved bill. True to its name, the bird nests in cacti—sharp needles don't seem to bother it as it builds its nest and raises its young in clusters of spines so dense that no predator dares approach too closely. Unfortunately, Cactus Wren populations seem to be in decline.

The wren's distinctive churring song is often used as a background sound in movies to evoke a desolate and lonesome atmosphere.

Cardinalis sinuatus

A close relative of the Northern Cardinal, the Pyrrhuloxia is a gray and crested desert specialist. The roots of the bird's odd name *(pyrrhula* and *loxia)* mean "flame colored" and "crooked" and refer to the red markings on its face, crest, and breast and its smashed-in bill. Huge flocks containing thousands of Pyrrhuloxias are sometimes seen in the winter—some of the birds remain in their breeding territories all year, while others migrate.

The Pyrrhuloxia's song can be loud and dramatic; it somewhat resembles the Northern Cardinal's *wooeat-wooeat-wooeat.* During the breeding season, males often engage in vigorous vocal competitions for the attention of females.

Pipilo fuscus

A common bird of southwestern deserts, the Canyon Towhee is a mixture of brown, buff, and gray with a rust-colored cap. At one time, the Canyon Towhee and California Towhee were considered a single species: the Brown Towhee. It usually doesn't take too long to find one hopping through the underbrush or scratching on the ground in search of seeds or insects. The towhee will sometimes come to feeding stations for cracked corn or peanuts.

At sunrise, you can often hear the Canyon Towhee's piping song, which is usually written as *chili, chili, chili* and is mixed with separate, sharp notes.

23. Black-crested Titmouse *Baeolophus atricristatus*

I t is a relief from the midday heat to ascend into Texas desert mountain ranges and rest in the shade of spreading oaks. Here the Black-crested Titmouse sings a simple and repetitive song throughout much of the day. Like the related Tufted Titmouse (once considered the same species), the Black-crested Titmouse sounds a plaintive *pootee-pootee-pootee* song with a slight difference in inflection and tone. The bird's upturned black crest and whitish forehead patch distinguish it from the eastern species, however.

After the breeding season, the Black-crested Titmouse moves in mixed-species flocks, often with chickadees and other birds. The titmouse is a regular visitor to backyard feeders.

Small and plainly dressed in olive gray, the Hutton's Vireo does not immediately draw attention. When it sings, however, its presence quickly becomes apparent. This species learns a few simple notes and repeats them many, many times before switching to others. If a neighboring male sings a different note, a defending male may quickly imitate the neighbor in reply.

The Hutton's Vireo more closely resembles the Ruby-crowned Kinglet than it does other vireos. And it shares the kinglet's nervous mannerisms, including regular wing flicking. It's a bit larger than the kinglet, however, with a thicker bill and slightly different wing markings.

O ut in the flat expanses of desert grassland and scrub, the Cassin's Sparrow can be heard singing from a low bush or during its short and low song-flights. But this species may be difficult to see unless males are engaging in their spectacular courtship displays—which involve skylarking flights and dramatic plummets with wings held wide open. The bird's sweet song carries far and ends with two distinct phrases.

During most of the year, the Cassin's Sparrow quietly searches the ground for seeds and insects, its drab gray-brown plumage hiding its presence from all but the most careful observer.

26. Lucy's Warbler

Vermivora luciae

The Lucy's Warbler earns the nickname "mesquite warbler" by nesting in desert washes choked with mesquite and other thorny brush. In ideal habitat, the bird can be locally quite common, and it's a treat to listen to its crisp song while waiting for a glimpse of its distinctive reddish crown. That bit of color stands out against the overall gray color of the bird's plumage.

Tiny and active, the Lucy's Warbler is the only warbler that lives in the desert. It was named in 1861 to honor the thirteen-year-old daughter of Spencer F. Baird, who later became secretary of the Smithsonian Institution.

The most common thrasher in the desert southwest is the Curve-billed Thrasher, a gray-brown bird with golden eyes and a long, black, curved bill. An inhabitant of dry brushlands, the bird spends most of its time on the ground, foraging for insects and seeds and occasionally berries and cactus fruits. The species' recent population decline is of great concern to scientists and bird lovers, who are working to preserve its preferred habitat from development.

The Curve-billed Thrasher's song is a series of phrases somewhat similar to that of its cousin the Northern Mockingbird. The sound is well known to those who live within the bird's range. For many Southwest residents, the thrasher is a backyard bird.

28. Painted Redstart

Myioborus pictus

O n a hot, sunny day, the sycamore-shaded canyons of desert mountains are a welcome retreat. In these forests, the Painted Redstart
offers regular entertainment—seemingly always in motion, this warbler dances and flashes as it scours tree trunks and branches for tiny insects
and spiders. Drooping the wings and fanning the tail are common redstart
habits. The bird's name derives from the Old German word *rothstert*, which
means "red tail," although its overall black plumage is contrasted with
white and orange highlights, not red.

The Painted Redstart's song is highly variable, but it's most always
sweet and clear and reaches a sudden stop.

29. Mexican Jay   *Aphelocoma ultramarina*

Most wooded habitats have a resident jay species. In the oak savannah woodlands of Arizona and New Mexico, it's the Mexican Jay, a large, active bird with a blue head, wings, and tail; bluish gray back; and grayish white breast. Unlike the similiar Western Scrub Jay, the Mexican Jay's throat and breast are unmarked. Like the Acorn Woodpecker, the jay stores acorns to eat when food is in short supply.

The Mexican Jay is a social creature—if you find one, you'll usually find a small flock working the oaks and keeping in constant vocal contact with each other. The bird's call is harsh with a slight downward inflection.

High above the oaks we hear a scream. We are being watched from above by a circling Zone-tailed Hawk, which is warning us away from its nearby nest. This hawk is known for its physical resemblance to a Turkey Vulture. It's thought that by mimicking the common and harmless carrion eater, the Zone-tailed Hawk might better approach unwary live prey, which is often lizards and snakes.

Zone-tailed Hawks live in the southwestern United States, Mexico, and Central America. During the winter, they virtually disappear from this country. The Zone-tailed Hawk's call is a harsh squeal somewhat similar to a Red-tailed Hawk's.

31. Acorn Woodpecker   *Melanerpes formicivora*

There's nothing like watching a group of Acorn Woodpeckers for good birding entertainment. This large, black bird with a red cap and distinctive "clown face" spends much of its time drilling storage holes in an appropriate wooden surface in order to store the acorns it collects. Some of these enormous granaries can hold tens of thousands of acorns. The bird also spends much time chasing others within its large family group—in their first two or three years, Acorn Woodpecker fledglings help raise their siblings, forming a complicated social organization.

The Acorn Woodpecker's call is a raucous laughing that befits its outgoing personality. Its drumming is a steady roll.

Callipepla californica

nother famous western entertainer is the California Quail, a popular game bird and the official state bird of California. During the nonbreeding season, huge coveys of these chunky ground dwellers can be seen chasing through the underbrush, tiny feet racing and distinctive head-top crests bobbing. Fast in flight, the quail is even faster on the ground. Its run has been clocked at close to twelve miles an hour. Unlike the related Bobwhite Quail, the California Quail roosts in bushes and shrubs.

During courtship, the male quail uses an elevated perch to broadcast his song, which sounds somewhat like a drawn-out honk.

The California Towhee is a drab brown bird that is content to skulk along the woodland floor, where it searches for insects and seeds while avoiding the attention of predators. A common western bird, the towhee favors backcountry forests, but it has been seen in wooded suburban settings. The bird is nonmigratory, although it does shift habitats, usually to differing elevations, to follow its food supply. The small population of "Inyo" California Towhees that is limited to the Argus Mountains in central California has been added to the threatened species list.

The California Towhee's song is a crisp series of accelerating *tsip* sounds.

D espite its colorful name, the Orange-crowned Warbler is one of the plainest in the warbler family. Its plumage is an overall drab olive gray, its breast is faintly streaked, and its namesake crown is often invisible—it's most often seen when the bird is agitated and the tiny head feathers are raised. Orange-crowned Warblers are common in California oak woodlands as well as the Gambel's oak-covered foothills of the lower Rockies. Unlike many other warbler species, orange-crown populations appear to be stable or increasing.

The bird's descending, twittering song sounds a bit different between coastal and inland intermountain birds, reflecting a slight subspecies variation.

35. Anna's Hummingbird

Yes, Anna's Hummingbirds do sing, and their scratchy, high-pitched songs seem to match their size and habits. The male Anna's Hummingbird, distinguished by its iridescent red gorget and hood, will find a bare twig overlooking a flower patch to use as both song perch and lookout as it guards its territory from trespassing rivals. During courtship, the male engages in a dramatic diving flight away from and then toward a female.

Anna's Hummingbirds tend to follow food sources throughout the year. It is the only hummingbird species that spends the winter primarily in the United States, and its population seems to be expanding.

The Black-headed Grosbeak has one of the richest and more beautiful songs of western songbirds. Although confused by some with the song of the American Robin, the grosbeak's song has a more robust tone and dances through the musical scales to higher and lower notes than the robin's does. Another clue: The robin tends to sing from the top of a tree while the grosbeak sings from a more hidden perch in the forest canopy.

The two birds don't really look alike, either. The Black-headed Grosbeak has a short, thick bill characteristic of all grosbeaks; the male has a black head, orangish underparts, and black-and-white–striped wings.

Woodland meadows and creekside riparian thickets are where we find the Fox Sparrow, a species that has been divided into four major types according to habitat and appearance. Two of these types—the Large-billed Fox Sparrow of the West Coast and the Slate-colored Fox Sparrow of the Rocky Mountains—nest in the western United States. Both sport contrasting gray and reddish plumage and have similar habits.

Larger than most sparrows, the Fox Sparrow spends much of its time on the ground, where it scratches and digs determinedly for food. Its rich up-and-down song is highly changeable; males rarely sing the exact same sequence twice.

The handsome Mountain Quail can be difficult to find. It usually stays hidden in mountain thickets, living quietly in small coveys. All that changes during courtship, however, when the single-note call of the male rings through the mountains. The male also sings as it spreads its wings and lifts its tail to woo a mate. The quail's head plumes indicate its mood—the feathers stand upright when the bird is agitated and lie flat when it's fearful.

The largest quail in North America, the Mountain Quail rarely flies. It prefers to run for cover if it feels threatened. Its migration, up and down mountain slopes, is done on foot, too.

A nother secretive resident of high western mountains is the Lincoln's Sparrow, which prefers wet and boggy thickets nestled in the montane forest. Hard to differentiate from the Swamp Sparrow and Song Sparrow, which are almost identical to it, the Lincoln's Sparrow has a fine-streaked, buff-colored breast. The species was named by John James Audubon in honor of his colleague Thomas Lincoln. It can be coaxed to feed on the ground beneath backyard feeders.

The Lincoln's Sparrow's song is an enchanting and delicate jumble of notes, in contrast to its nondescript brown and gray plumage. It will occasionally sing while in flight.

The expansive blue skies over rugged western highlands and northern deserts are reflected in the plumage of the Mountain Bluebird. This colorful cavity-nesting thrush is a common sight over much of its range. It can usually be seen perched or hovering over a clearing, scanning for insect prey on the ground. Unlike its eastern counterpart, the Mountain Bluebird has longer wings and a trimmer build and so can hover more easily. It also sports a pale blue chin and breast; the Eastern Bluebird's are reddish.

The Mountain Bluebird's song is a simple, echoing whistle. Most of the birds migrate to the Southwest for the winter.

The large and handsome Western Gull is a conspicuous character along the Pacific coast. The bird requires four years to achieve its adult appearance—white head and breast with slate-gray and black wings, a flat forehead, and big bill—and may live to be twenty. Western Gulls prefer to nest in offshore breeding colonies where there is less risk of predation; these colonies are most often in California or Oregon waters. Like most gulls, the bird will scavenge food if wild prey is not available.

Western Gulls make a whistled *keow* call, a familiar sound along ocean beaches and docks in the summer.

42. Black Oystercatcher   *Haematopus bachmani*

A tide pool specialist, the handsome Black Oystercatcher is a favorite permanent resident of the rocky Pacific Ocean coastline. The bird might have been better named the "limpetprier" or "mussellcracker," however, since these more accurately reflect its dining habits. An unmistakable all-black bird with yellow eyes, pink legs, and a heavy red bill, it rarely eats oysters.

Spring is a time of hectic flight chases and excited, ringing calling as pairs of Black Oystercatchers form and territories are reestablished on the beach. Oil spills, habitat depletion, and nesting disturbances have all had an effect on oystercatcher populations, which are in worrisome decline.

M oist Pacific Northwest rain forests nearly always host a nesting pair of Pacific-slope Flycatchers. These small birds forage for flying insects by perching in the midcanopy and then making short flights to snap up their prey. Its nest frequently includes man-made items such as paper and string.

With its greenish-brown back and yellowish underbelly, the Pacific-slope Flycatcher looks like most other Empidonax flycatchers. In fact, its species name refers to the difficulty even experts have identifying it in the field. The bird's squeaky, three-part song is just about the only way to distinguish it from the Cordilleran Flycatcher, once considered part of the same species.

*D*own from starlit skies comes a twittering, first from here, then from there. It's long before dawn, and a flock of Violet-green Swallows is high in the sky, roving for flying insects and making a twittering *chee-chee-chee.* It's a common sound along streams, riverways, and windblown ridges throughout the bird's large western range. Rarely seen alone, the bird is often found in mixed flocks with other swallow species.

The Violet-green Swallow sports a bright, white underside and face that contrasts with its bronzish-green back and head. It has a notched tail, and its flight can seem stiff and wobbly.

One of the first birds that visitors to western forests notice is the dramatically outfitted Steller's Jay. Mistakenly called a "blue jay" by some, this bird is a richer blue than the Blue Jay of the East. Its crested head and back are a blackish brown. Like most jays, the Steller's Jay has an inquisitive and raucous personality. It makes a variety of calls, most of them harsh and raspy.

The Steller's Jay is nonmigratory, although birds that live in higher elevations will move to lower spots in the winter. Flocks of jays often "irrupt" into areas that have a plentiful food supply.

The gray and orange Varied Thrush is a bird of dark, shady, damp Northwest forests, at home in old-growth conifers that have stood for centuries. The bird is secretive, and its beautiful colors can be surprisingly difficult to see amid the dappled sunlight that filters down through spruce boughs. The thrush aggressively defends its territory, often flashing the patterned underside of its tail and its wings and back at an intruder.

The Varied Thrush's drawn-out single-note song has a somewhat eerie quality. The male will engage in a long bout of singing from one perch, then fly to another and sing again.

The Wilson's Warbler is a common summer resident of moist, brushy habitats throughout boreal Canada and Alaska and south into the montane and coastal western United States. Watch for the male's yellow face and undersides, drab back, and jet black cap as it hops through the underbrush. The tiny bird was named for Alexander Wilson, one of the first ornithologists in North America. Studies indicate that the species' population seems to be in decline, perhaps because of the logging of its nesting grounds and parasitism by the Brown-headed Cowbird.

The Wilson's Warbler's simple, chattering song goes downward in pitch and is not known for its melodiousness.

48. Song Sparrow　　　*Melospiza melodia*

One of the most common sounds along western waterways is the bright song of the Song Sparrow. This bird is not shy about performing long bouts of singing and defending its patch of willows from aggressive neighbors. Almost any wet habitat will do; the bird is also found in wetland marshes and coastal estuaries, often in or near developed areas. The Song Sparrow's streaky chest and central breast spot help distingush it from other sparrow species. The song of the Song Sparrow features two or three distinct introductory notes, almost as though the bird were clearing its throat. Variable shorter notes and trills follow.

The Willow Flycatcher is found throughout much of the northern United States, but it is restricted to moist habitats, usually along streams, ponds, and wetlands. The bird shows a preference for slightly more open spaces than do other flycatchers, although it's still a challenge to differentiate the Willow Flycatcher from the nearly identical Alder Flycatcher in the field. The bird will work hard to drive other flycatchers out of its territory.

The Willow Flycatcher's staccato *fitz-bew!* song is a helpful identification clue, and it will often sing anytime day or night from an exposed perch, which it will occupy for some time.

50. Common Yellowthroat   *Geothlypis trichas*

The Common Yellowthroat, perhaps more than any of its warbler cousins, has adopted marshes and wetland brushy tangles as home. The male's black face mask contrasting with its dramatic yellow throat make this beautiful bird unmistakable. The bird is more often heard than seen, however. Its distinctive *witchity-witchity* song is a familiar sound in wetlands across a large part of the country.

Yellowthroat populations appear to be holding steady, even though the Brown-headed Cowbird often lays its eggs in yellowthroat nests; cowbird chicks then outcompete the smaller chicks when they hatch. The Common Yellowthroat is also a frequent target of raptor attacks.

Always in motion, always chattering or singing its choppy song day and night, the Marsh Wren is a signature species of almost any stand of cattails or bulrushes. Like most wrens, the bird is seemingly afraid of nothing and will defend its territory vigorously. Marsh Wrens sport dark caps and white eyebrow stripes and have the distinctive, jaunty wren tail. Experts are considering whether western and eastern Marsh Wrens are actually separate species.

This wren is a master at assembling a choppy jumble of sounds into a barrage so complex that only by slowing it down can we appreciate the bird's virtuosity.

Xanthocephalus xanthocephalus

A breeding colony of Yellow-headed Blackbirds puts on quite a show—a jumble of blazing yellow heads, jet-black bodies, and a flash of white in the wings. The accompanying sound track adds to the excitement; it's hard to believe that such screeching, grinding, and yelping can come from an animal, much less a beautiful songbird. The cacophony that rises from many cattail marshes tests the limit of what we call birdsong.

Larger than the Red-winged Blackbird, the Yellow-headed Blackbird often drives these relatives out of prime nesting areas. Males set up nests with a number of females but generally help to feed only the first brood.

53. Wilson's Snipe

Gallinago delicata

The Wilson's Snipe, formerly known as the Common Snipe, is one of the largest shorebirds, cryptically colored to hide in the brown vegetation of a marsh. The bird is equipped with a long, thin bill perfect for probing deep into soft mud for food. It can actually open just the tip of its bill, keeping the rest closed.

In the spring, it may be easier to find a Wilson's Snipe by sound. Prolonged calling and noisy, winnowing flight advertise its home. The bird breeds in the northern United States and Canada; it migrates to southern states and Mexico in the winter.

S trikingly attractive and elegant, the American Avocet often forages in shallow inland mudflats by dipping its bill underwater and sweeping it from side to side. That bill—long, delicate, slender, and upturned—is the bird's most distinctive feature, although the avocet's bold black-and-white plumage is a key identifier, too.

The American Avocet is a social bird, although at times the bickering and chasing that goes on within a colony during the breeding season hardly seems civil. Its shrill, agitated call is most noticeable at this time. Nesting is done inland; the bird usually flies to coastal waters in the nonbreeding season.

Western wetlands and the open countryside are often patrolled by Northern Harriers. These raptors have long tails and wings that help them float low over the ground and surprise a variety of prey, including rodents, small birds, frogs, and snakes. Unique feather patterns create pronounced facial disks that give the harrier an owl-like appearance and exceptional hearing abilities, allowing it to detect small creatures moving unseen through the grass.

The Northern Harrier emits a sharp chatter and a piercing scream. Males often mate with more than one female and so spend much of the breeding season hunting for food to bring to their young.

The term "shorebird" applies to the Long-billed Curlew only during the nonbreeding season, when the bird winters on Pacific shores. The bird's extended, curved bill is bad news for tiny shrimp hiding deep in their burrows. When spring arrives, curlews move away from the coast into western grasslands, where they often feast on earthworms. In their breeding territory, they begin long, slow, circling display flights and haunting, mournful calls as part of their mating rituals.

Long-billed Curlew populations were almost decimated by farm plowing and hunting in the early twentieth century. Even today, the curlew's population is small and on the decline.

L
ong-billed Dowitchers migrate to the far northwestern reaches of the arctic tundra each year for early summer nesting. By late summer, they have returned to coastal mudflats, where small flocks probe for food with a motion that looks like a sewing machine. The bird will occasionally put its whole head underwater. It feeds deliberately, walking slowly between probes, rarely running. Unlike the Short-billed Dowitcher, which looks quite similar, the Long-Billed Dowitcher prefers freshwater feeding grounds. In the breeding season, the bird is grayish on top, orangish underneath.

The dowitcher's call is a *peep* given alone or in a series.

58. Northern Pintail   *Anas acuta*

The Northern Pintail is a classy looking bird, finely proportioned and stately colored. A breeding resident throughout a large part of the northern United States, Canada, and Alaska, it even reaches tundra ponds near the Arctic Circle, nesting farther north than nearly any other North American duck. Long, thin tail feathers—obvious in flight and when the duck is in the water—give the bird its name. Pintails spend the winter in large flocks, sometimes mixing with other ducks. Because it's so wary, it can be hard to approach.

Male Northern Pintails give quick trilling calls on their nesting grounds.

Oxyura jamaicensis

O ne can hardly watch a Ruddy Duck without a bit of a smile. Its somewhat goofy blue bill and erect tail seem comical, an impression only reinforced when the male makes its sputtering call during a head-bobbing courtship display made during breeding season. The duck, named for the male's reddish body, sports distinctive white cheek patches throughout the year. It nests in prairie potholes throughout western states.

The Ruddy Duck's breeding behaviors have gotten it into trouble in England. Because it interbreeds so successfully with many European duck species, the British decided in 2003 to cull the country's entire population of these American invaders.

60. Canada Goose   *Branta canadensis*

There is a restlessness in the autumn air, chilly winds release leaves into flight, frost crunches underfoot, and a small group of Canada Geese presses southward. Wings whistling and voices honking, these birds presage the coming winter; come March, however, they will return heralding a new spring and a renewal of life. For many, the familiar honk of the Canada Goose is the sound of bird migration.

Common across most of the country, the geese are becoming tame in some places, remaining over winter on their spring breeding grounds. But most Canada Geese still migrate, flying noisily across the sky in their distinctive Vs.

Master List of CD Contents

Species numbers throughout the book are equivalent to the track numbers on the compact disc.

1. Mountain Chickadee
2. Pine Siskin
3. Red-breasted Nuthatch
4. Downy Woodpecker
5. Red-naped Sapsucker
6. Warbling Vireo
7. Yellow-rumped Warbler
8. Western Tanager
9. White-crowned Sparrow
10. Lazuli Bunting
11. Dusky Flycatcher
12. Hermit Thrush
13. Yellow Warbler
14. Western Meadowlark
15. Brewer's Sparrow
16. Sage Sparrow
17. Bewick's Wren
18. Lark Sparrow
19. Horned Lark
20. Cactus Wren
21. Pyrrhuloxia
22. Canyon Towhee
23. Black-crested Titmouse
24. Hutton's Vireo
25. Cassin's Sparrow
26. Lucy's Warbler
27. Curve-billed Thrasher
28. Painted Redstart
29. Mexican Jay
30. Zone-tailed Hawk
31. Acorn Woodpecker
32. California Quail
33. California Towhee
34. Orange-crowned Warbler
35. Anna's Hummingbird
36. Black-headed Grosbeak
37. Fox Sparrow
38. Mountain Quail
39. Lincoln's Sparrow
40. Mountain Bluebird
41. Western Gull
42. Black Oystercatcher
43. Pacific-slope Flycatcher
44. Violet-green Swallow
45. Steller's Jay
46. Varied Thrush
47. Wilson's Warbler
48. Song Sparrow
49. Willow Flycatcher
50. Common Yellowthroat
51. Marsh Wren
52. Yellow-headed Blackbird
53. Wilson's Snipe
54. American Avocet
55. Northern Harrier
56. Long-billed Curlew
57. Long-billed Dowitcher
58. Northern Pintail
59. Ruddy Duck
60. Canada Goose